Magic Coffee:

Bewitching Aromas to Awaken Your Senses

Kris Roots

Creative Consciousness Editions   Kris Roots

TABLE OF CONTENTS

Introduction

Precautions

- Spices
- Alcohols
- Herbs
- Citrus fruits
- Flavoured syrups or natural extracts
- Dried fruits
- Complementary flavours
- Milk and plant-based alternatives: creative textures and flavours

Caffeinated desserts and delicacies

Explore coffee cultures around the world

Iconic enhanced coffees from different regions

Creative Consciousness Editions   Kris Roots

Traditions and rituals associated with coffee in various countries

Discover local cafes on trips

Thanks

Creative Consciousness Editions   Kris Roots

INTRODUCTION

Dear reader,

In a world where every cup of coffee is an experience to be savored, it's time to immerse yourself in a captivating universe of flavors, aromas and discoveries. Welcome to "Magic Coffee: Bewitching Aromas to Awaken Your Senses", an exciting journey through the art of coffee enhancement. In these pages, we invite you to explore the secrets to turn your ordinary cup of coffee into an extraordinary creation.

Spices: Let the spices awaken your senses by discovering the exquisite combinations that sublimate coffee. Notes of cinnamon, cardamom, nutmeg and many more will transport you to a world of spicy delights.

Spirits: Discover how carefully selected spirits can blend harmoniously with coffee to create intoxicating cocktails. From liqueurs to whisky to exotic spirits, explore the bold marriages that will give your coffee a whole new dimension.

Aromatic herbs: Dive into a fragrant garden where aromatic herbs mingle with coffee. Notes of fresh mint, basil, rosemary and many more will invite you to an unforgettable sensory experience.

Citrus fruits: Discover how citrus fruits can brighten up your cup of coffee with their vibrant freshness. Bursts of orange, lemon, grapefruit and other citrus fruits will make you discover tangy and revitalizing flavors.

Flavoured syrups and natural extracts: Explore an endless palette of flavours by adding flavoured syrups and natural extracts to your coffee. Vanilla, caramel, almond, and many more, these liquid sweets will delight your taste buds.

Dried fruits: Add a crunchy and succulent touch to your coffee by incorporating dried fruit. From roasted almonds to dried figs, discover how these natural delicacies go perfectly with coffee.

Complementary flavours: Immerse yourself in the art of taste balance by exploring complementary flavours that can elevate your coffee to new heights. Bold and harmonious combinations await you, where the sweet meets the salty, and the bitter dances with the sweet.

Milk and plant-based alternatives: Discover how choosing milk or plant-based alternatives can transform your coffee. From the creamy sweetness of cow's milk to the nutty delights of almond milk, explore the endless possibilities available to you.

Creative Consciousness Editions   Kris Roots

Caffeinated desserts and delicacies: Immerse yourself in a world of sweet delights by discovering desserts and delicacies that go perfectly with coffee. From tiramisus to brownies to affogatos, these treats will delight your taste buds.

Explore coffee cultures around the world: Discover fascinating coffee-related cultures around the world. Explore the rituals, traditions and legends that make coffee a symbol of conviviality and sharing.

Iconic Enhanced Coffees from Different Regions: Immerse yourself in iconic Enhanced Coffees from various parts of the world. From Turkish coffee to Vietnamese coffee, discover the unique preparations and distinctive flavors for which they are famous.

Traditions and rituals associated with coffee in various countries: Soak up the mesmerizing traditions and rituals that surround coffee drinking in different countries. From the Ethiopian coffee ceremony to the meticulous preparation of Italian coffee, explore the unique practices that give this drink cultural depth.

Discover local cafes on trips: Go on an adventure and discover local cafes on your travels. From lively street cafes to trendy cafes, immerse yourself in the vibrant atmosphere and sample regional flavors that will make every experience an unforgettable memory.

Immerse yourself in the magical world of enhanced coffees and let yourself be transported by mesmerizing aromas, captivating flavors and unexpected taste discoveries. Get ready to awaken your senses and redefine your relationship with this beloved drink. Welcome to "Magic Coffee: Bewitching Aromas to Awaken Your Senses

Kris Roots

PRECAUTIONS

Allergies and sensitivities : It is important to mention that some people may be allergic or sensitive to certain ingredients used to enhance coffee. For example, nuts, such as almonds or hazelnuts, are often used to flavor coffees, but they can trigger allergic reactions in some people. It is therefore recommended to always indicate the ingredients used and advise readers to exercise caution if they have known allergies.

Caffeine intolerance : It is essential to remind readers that coffee contains caffeine, which can have stimulating effects on the central nervous system. People who are sensitive to caffeine, such as those with sleep problems or gastrointestinal sensitivity, should be advised to moderate their intake or opt for decaffeinated alternatives.

Effects of alcohol blends : If your book offers recipes for improved coffees containing alcohol, it is essential to emphasize the precautions associated with responsible alcohol consumption. It is important to remind readers not to exceed the recommended limits for alcohol consumption and not to drive after consuming alcoholic beverages.

Drug interactions : Some ingredients used to enhance coffee, such as herbs or natural extracts, may interact with certain medications. Readers who take medications regularly are advised to consult their healthcare professional to check for potential interactions between coffee ingredients and their medications.

Moderate consumption : Although enhanced coffee can provide a pleasant taste experience, it is important to remind readers to consume these beverages in moderation. Excessive caffeine consumption can lead to side effects such as restlessness, insomnia, increased heart rate, and gastrointestinal problems.

Pregnancy and breast-feeding: It is recommended to mention that pregnant or breastfeeding women should be cautious when consuming caffeine, as high amounts can have effects on fetal development or be transmitted to the infant through breast milk. It is best to consult a medical professional for specific advice on caffeine consumption during this time.

Sugar content: Some enhanced coffees may contain high amounts of added sugar or flavored syrups, which can be of concern for people with diabetes, weight problems, or looking to reduce their sugar intake. It is recommended to offer less sweet alternatives, such as the use of natural sweeteners or low-sugar syrups, and to encourage moderate consumption.

Hydration : Caffeine can have a diuretic effect, which means it can increase urine production and contribute to dehydration if consumed in excessive amounts. It is important to remind readers to maintain adequate hydration by also drinking water and avoid relying solely on coffee for their daily fluid intake.

Ingredient quality : When recommending spices, syrups, extracts, or other ingredients to enhance coffee, it's important to emphasize the importance of using high-quality ingredients from trusted sources. This ensures not only a better flavor, but also food safety, avoiding expired or questionable quality products.

Proper preparation : Be sure to include clear instructions on how to brew and serve improved coffees safely and hygienically. This may include advice on food handling, proper storage of ingredients, and use of clean equipment.

SPICES

Cinnamon : Cinnamon adds a warm, slightly sweet flavor to coffee. You can sprinkle a small amount of ground cinnamon into your cup of coffee or add a cinnamon stick during the brewing process.

Cardamom: Cardamom is a popular spice in Middle Eastern cafes. It adds a fragrant and slightly spicy note to the coffee. You can add crushed cardamom seeds during brewing or use cardamom powder.

Nutmeg : A pinch of freshly grated nutmeg can give your coffee a delicate and subtle flavor.

Creative Consciousness Editions   Kris Roots

Ginger : Ginger brings a spicy and pungent flavor. You can grate fresh ginger into your coffee or add a small amount of ground ginger.

Star Anise : Star anise adds a slightly sweet and aniseed flavor to coffee. You can add a star anise to your cup during brewing.

Cloves : Cloves add a warm, slightly sweet and spicy flavor. Add one or two cloves to your ground coffee before brewing your coffee.

Black pepper : A pinch of ground black pepper can add a slight touch of spice and complexity to your coffee. Add it directly to your cup of coffee or infuser.

Black cardamom: Black cardamom has a more intense and smoky flavor than green cardamom. You can crush the black cardamom seeds and add them to your coffee before brewing.

Turmeric : Turmeric is a spice with an earthy and slightly bitter taste. Add a pinch of powdered turmeric to your coffee to give it a subtle note.

Cayenne pepper : If you like bold flavors, you can add a small pinch of cayenne pepper to your coffee for a touch of spicy heat.

Nutmeg : Just like nutmeg, a pinch of freshly grated nutmeg can add a delicate, slightly sweet flavor to your coffee.

Green Cardamom: Green cardamom is a very aromatic spice that adds a fresh, slightly lemony note to coffee. You can crush a few green cardamom seeds and add them to your ground coffee before brewing your coffee.

Allspice: Also known as "allspice", allspice has a complex flavor reminiscent of the mixture of cinnamon, cloves and nutmeg. Add a small amount of ground allspice to your coffee for an exotic flavor.

Anise : Anise adds a mild, slightly sweet flavor to coffee. You can add a small amount of anise seeds to your ground coffee before brewing.

Creative Consciousness Editions   Kris Roots

Madagascar Cardamom: Madagascar cardamom is a different variety from green cardamom, with a milder and sweeter flavor. Crush a few Madagascar cardamom seeds and add them to your coffee for a touch of delicate aroma.

Remember to start with small amounts of spices and adjust according to your personal taste. Experiment with different combinations to discover the one you like the most.

ALCOHOLS

There are many alcohols that you can add to your coffee to give it a touch of aroma and flavor. Here are some popular suggestions:

Rum : Rum is often used to flavor coffee. You can add a small amount of brown rum or spiced rum to your coffee. Make sure you choose a quality rum that matches your flavor preferences.

Whisky : A little whiskey can add a robust and warm note to your coffee. Whiskies with a peated or smoky taste can bring an extra dimension to the drink. Experiment with different types of whiskey, like bourbon, scotch or Irish whiskey, to find the one you like the most.

Coffee-based liqueurs: There are many coffee-based liqueurs on the market, such as Kahlúa, Tia Maria or Café Patron. These liqueurs are specially designed to be mixed with coffee and can add notes of coffee, chocolate or vanilla to your drink.

Amaretto : Amaretto is an almond-based liqueur with a sweet and slightly bitter flavor. Add a dash to your coffee for a touch of sweet almond.

Cream of whisky : Cream of whisky, like Baileys Irish Cream, is a creamy, sweet liquor that pairs very well with coffee. It adds a creamy texture and slightly sweet flavor to your drink.

Brandy : Brandy can add a rich, fruity flavor to your coffee. You can opt for traditional brandy or try flavored variations, like orange brandy.

Grand Marnier : This is a cognac and orange liqueur that adds a citrus flavor and mild bitterness to your coffee.

Frangelico : This hazelnut-based Italian liqueur adds a sweet and subtle nutty flavor to your coffee.

Mint cream : If you like refreshing flavors, adding a small amount of spearmint or white mint cream to your coffee can give it a minty touch.

Amaretto di Saronno : A variant of the traditional amaretto, Amaretto di Saronno is an Italian liqueur that offers a richer and more complex almond flavor.

Chartreuse: Chartreuse is a French herbal liqueur with a unique and herbaceous taste. It can add an interesting note to your coffee.

Sambuca : Sambuca is an aniseed Italian liqueur that brings a mild and distinct flavor to your coffee.

Cocoa cream : For a chocolate twist, you can add cocoa cream to your coffee. It adds a sweet and creamy chocolate flavor.

Irish whiskey: Irish whiskey is known to be soft and velvety. Adding it to your coffee can give a warm and slightly spicy flavor.

Cointreau : This is a French orange liqueur that brings a sweet and fragrant citrus flavor to your coffee.

Hazelnut cream : This hazelnut-flavored liqueur adds a deliciously sweet and nutty flavor to your coffee.

Coconut cream : For a tropical twist, add a little coconut cream to your coffee for a creamy and exotic flavor.

William pear : This pear liqueur offers a fruity and sweet flavor that goes well with coffee.

Almond liqueur : If you like the flavor of almond, add almond liquor to your coffee for a sweet, fragrant flavor.

Blackcurrant cream : Blackcurrant cream is a blackcurrant-based liqueur that can add a fruity and slightly tangy note to your coffee.

Raspberry cream : This raspberry liqueur adds a fruity and sweet flavor to your coffee, with a slight acidity.

Pisco : Pisco is a grape brandy native to Peru and Chile. Its unique and aromatic taste can bring an interesting touch to your coffee.

Banana cream : If you like banana flavors, add a little banana cream to your coffee for a touch of fruity sweetness.

Keep in mind that adding alcohol to your coffee can increase its alcohol content. Drink in moderation and adjust the amounts according to your personal preferences.

HERBS

Aromatic herbs can bring an interesting touch to your coffee. Here are some suggestions for herbs you can try:

Mint : Adding a few fresh mint leaves to your coffee can give it a refreshing, slightly minty flavor.

Rosemary : A small sprig of rosemary added to your coffee can bring a woody and fragrant note. Be sure to crush it lightly to release the aromas before adding it.

Basil: Basil is an aromatic herb that can add a touch of freshness and subtle aroma to your

Creative Consciousness Editions   Kris Roots

coffee. Add a few fresh basil leaves to your cup of coffee.

Lavender : Lavender can give your coffee a delicate floral flavor. Use dried culinary lavender flowers and add them in moderation to avoid too strong a flavor.

Thyme : Thyme is an aromatic herb that can bring an earthy, slightly lemony note to your coffee. Add a small sprig of fresh thyme to your cup of coffee.

Tarragon: Tarragon is an aromatic herb with a subtly aniseed flavor. Adding a few sprigs of fresh tarragon to your coffee can give it a unique touch of aroma.

Herbes de Provence : This herbal blend including rosemary, thyme, oregano and savory can be added to your coffee for a distinct Mediterranean flavor. Use a small amount of the mixture to avoid saturating the coffee with flavors.

Sage leaves : Sage has an earthy, slightly peppery flavor. Adding a few fresh sage leaves to your coffee can give it an interesting herbaceous note.

Coriander leaves : Coriander has a fresh, lemony flavor. Adding a few fresh coriander leaves to your coffee can give it an exotic and refreshing flavor.

Thai basil leaves: Thai basil is a variety of basil with a distinctive, spicy aroma. Adding a few Thai basil leaves to your coffee can give it an exotic and fragrant flavor.

Lemongrass leaves: Lemongrass has a lemony and refreshing flavor. Adding a few sprigs of crushed lemongrass to your coffee can give it a fresh, aromatic note.

Vervain leaves : Vervain is an herb with a lemony and soothing flavor. Infusing a few verbena leaves into your coffee can give it a subtle and relaxing note.

Peppermint leaves : If you prefer a more peppery and intense mint flavor, adding peppermint leaves to your coffee can be a good option.

Lemon balm leaves : Lemon balm has a sweet, soothing lemon balm flavor. Adding a few fresh lemon balm leaves to your coffee can give it a delicate and relaxing note.

It's important to note that adding herbs to coffee can be a matter of personal preference and may require a bit of experimentation to find the combinations you like the most. Start with small amounts of herbs and adjust to taste.

CITRUS FRUITS

There are several citrus fruits that you can use to enhance your coffee with a fresh and tangy citrus note. Here are some suggestions:

Orange zest : Adding a little orange zest to your coffee can give it a subtle, fragrant citrus flavor. Be sure to use only the colored outer part of the bark, avoiding the bitter white part.

Lemon zest : Grated lemon zest can bring a tangy and refreshing touch to your coffee. Try adding a little fresh lemon zest to your cup of coffee.

Grapefruit zest : For a slightly more intense citrus flavor, add grapefruit zest to your coffee. It can give a lively and tangy note to your drink.

Lime zest : Lime zest can add a fresh, lemony flavor to your coffee. Try adding a small amount for a subtle touch of citrus.

Orange juice : If you prefer a more pronounced orange flavor, you can add a small amount of freshly squeezed orange juice to your coffee. This will add a sweet and juicy citrus note.

Tangerine : Tangerine zest or juice can bring a sweet and delicate flavor to your coffee. Try adding a small amount for a subtle citrus note.

Bergamot : Bergamot is a citrus fruit that is often paired with Earl Grey tea, but you can also experiment with its unique aroma in coffee. Add a few drops of bergamot oil or use brewed Earl Grey tea to brew your coffee.

Clementine : Clementine is a sweet and juicy citrus fruit. Add a few slices of fresh clementine to your cup of coffee for a refreshing citrus flavor.

Yuzu : Yuzu is a Japanese citrus fruit with a complex and tangy flavor. You can use yuzu juice or zest to add an exotic and refreshing note to your coffee.

Lime lime: Lime can bring a bright, tangy flavor to your coffee. Add a few drops of fresh lime juice for a touch of sparkling citrus fruits.

Pomelo: Pomelo is a tropical citrus fruit with a sweet and slightly bitter flavor. Add pieces of fresh pomelo to your coffee for a unique and refreshing flavor.

Combava : Combava is a citrus fruit native to Southeast Asia with an intense and lemony aroma. Use grated combava zest to brew your coffee and give it an exotic flavor.

Kumquat: Kumquats are small citrus fruits that can be eaten whole, including their skin. Add a few

Creative Consciousness Editions   Kris Roots

sliced kumquats to your coffee for a bright, tangy citrus flavor.

Lemon caviar: Lemon caviar, also known as finger lime, is an Australian citrus fruit with juicy little pearls inside. Pop a few lemon caviar pearls in your coffee for a unique taste experience.

Meyer Lemon : Meyer Lemon is a hybrid of lemon and orange with a sweet, fragrant flavor. Use Meyer lemon zest or juice to add a subtle citrus note to your coffee.

Satsuma mandarin : Satsuma mandarins are sweet and juicy citrus fruits. Add satsuma mandarin wedges to your coffee for a refreshing and sweet citrus flavor.

Don't forget to taste as you go and adjust the quantities according to your personal preferences. Citrus fruits can bring a touch of freshness and liveliness to your coffee, so have fun experimenting with different combinations to find the one you like the most.

Creative Consciousness Editions   Kris Roots

FLAVOURED SYRUPS OR NATURAL EXTRACTS

There is a wide variety of flavored syrups and natural extracts that you can add to your coffee to enhance it with additional flavors. Here are some suggestions:

Vanilla syrup : Vanilla syrup is a classic choice that adds sweetness and subtle flavor to your coffee.

Caramel syrup : Caramel syrup can give a sweet and caramelized note to your coffee, creating a gourmet flavor.

Almond syrup : Almond syrup can bring a delicate and slightly sweet flavor to your coffee, with characteristic almond notes.

Hazelnut syrup : Hazelnut syrup offers a sweet and rich nutty flavor that pairs well with coffee.

Chocolate syrup : For chocolate lovers, chocolate syrup can add a delicious chocolate note to your coffee, reminiscent of the flavors of a mocha.

Pumpkin Spice Syrup : If you like warm spice flavors, pumpkin spice syrup can be a great choice to add a fall flavor to your coffee.

Almond extract : Pure almond extract can be used to add a subtle almond flavor to your coffee. Use a few drops according to your personal taste.

Coconut extract : Coconut extract can give a tropical touch to your coffee, adding a creamy coconut flavor.

Mint extract : If you like refreshing flavors, mint extract can be added to your coffee for a pleasant minty note.

Maple syrup : Maple syrup adds a sweet and rich flavor to your coffee, reminiscent of the warm aromas of freshly poured maple syrup.

Coconut syrup : Coconut syrup can give an exotic and slightly sweet note to your coffee, bringing a tropical flavor.

Cinnamon syrup : Cinnamon syrup adds a warm, spicy flavor to your coffee, ideal for cinnamon lovers.

Salted Caramel Syrup : Salted caramel syrup combines the sweetness of caramel with a subtle hint of salt, creating a delicious balance in your coffee.

Smoked maple syrup : If you're looking for a more intense and distinctive flavour, smoked maple syrup can bring a subtle smoky note to your coffee.

Creative Consciousness Editions   Kris Roots

Orange extract : Pure orange extract can add a bright, fresh orange flavor to your coffee, reminiscent of citrus aromas.

Macadamia Nut Extract: Macadamia nut extract offers a rich, buttery flavor, bringing a delicate note of macadamia nuts to your coffee.

Lavender extract : If you enjoy floral flavors, lavender extract can bring a fragrant and subtle note to your coffee.

Pecan syrup : Pecan syrup offers a rich, deliciously nutty flavor that pairs well with coffee.

Biscotti syrup : Biscotti syrup adds notes of biscuit, almond and vanilla to your coffee, creating a gourmet tasting experience.

Bourbon Maple Syrup : This syrup combines the sweetness of maple with the rich, caramelized aromas of bourbon, adding a touch of elegance to your coffee.

Gingerbread syrup : Gingerbread syrup adds cinnamon, ginger, clove, and nutmeg flavors to your coffee, reminiscent of holiday season delights.

Toasted Coconut Syrup : This syrup offers a roasted, lightly caramelized coconut flavor that pairs well with coffee for a tropical experience.

Bitter Almond Extract : Bitter almond extract adds a deep, slightly bitter almond flavor to your coffee, providing a distinct note.

Cardamom extract: Cardamom extract brings a spicy, lemony and lightly peppery flavor to your coffee, adding a touch of exoticism.

Cashew extract : Cashew extract adds a buttery, slightly sweet flavor to your coffee, creating a unique combination.

These suggestions are simply examples and there are many other flavored syrups and natural extracts available on the market. Feel free to explore different options and experiment with combinations to find your preference when it comes to coffee flavor.

DRIED FRUITS

Here are some dried fruits you can consider adding to your coffee to improve it:

Almonds: Almonds add a crunchy texture and delicious nutty flavor to your coffee. You can use them whole, tapered or crushed.

Pecans : Pecans bring a rich, buttery flavor to your coffee. You can use them whole or crushed to add a touch of crunch.

Cashews : Cashews have a mild, creamy flavor that can complement coffee. Add them whole or chopped for an interesting texture.

Macadamia nuts: Macadamia nuts have a rich and delicate flavor that can add a touch of luxury to your coffee. You can use them whole or chopped.

Nuts : Walnuts, such as walnuts, pecans or Brazil nuts, bring an earthy flavor and crunchy texture to your coffee.

Pistachios: Pistachios can bring a slightly salty flavor and vibrant color to your coffee. Use chopped or whole them for an interesting taste experience.

Coconut : Grated or chipped coconut can add a tropical flavor and light texture to your coffee. It pairs well with softer coffees.

Raisins : Raisins can add natural sweetness and chewy texture to your coffee. Add a few raisins to your cup for a sweet touch.

Dates : Dates are naturally sweet and can add a rich, caramelized flavor to your coffee. Stone and chop a few dates to incorporate into your drink.

Dried figs : Dried figs have a sweet flavor and a slightly chewy texture that pairs well with coffee. Cut the dried figs into small pieces and add them to your cup of coffee.

Prunes : Prunes add natural sweetness and a slightly tart flavor to your coffee. Cut the prunes into small pieces and incorporate them into your drink.

Dried cranberries : Dried cranberries offer a tangy and slightly sweet flavor that can add a touch of freshness to your coffee. Add a few dried cranberries to your cup.

Dried coconut : Grated dried coconut can bring a tropical flavor and crunchy texture to your coffee. Sprinkle a small amount on top of your drink.

Pine nuts: Pine nuts have a delicate flavor and a slightly crunchy texture that can add a touch of sophistication to your coffee. Add a few to your cup.

Dried apricots: Dried apricots have a sweet flavor and a chewy texture. Add a few dried apricots cut into pieces to your coffee for a note of natural sweetness.

Agen prunes : Agen prunes are renowned for their sweet flavour and tender texture. Add a few chopped Agen prunes to your coffee for a touch of sweetness and richness.

Dried cherries: Dried cherries have a fruity and sweet flavor that can bring an extra dimension to your coffee. Add a few dried cherries to your cup for a deliciously sweet note.

Goji berries : Goji berries are known for their slightly sweet flavor and antioxidant benefits. Add a few goji berries to your coffee for a touch of sweetness and liveliness.

Dried pineapple: Dried pineapple offers a tropical and sweet flavor that can bring an exotic note to your coffee. Add a few pieces of dried pineapple for a refreshing taste.

Mixed dried fruits : For a variety of flavors, you can opt for a dried fruit blend that includes raisins, almonds, walnuts, hazelnuts, pecans, etc. Add a handful of this blend to your coffee for an explosion of flavors.

Dried mango: Dried mango offers a sweet and juicy flavor that can add a tropical touch to your coffee. Add a few pieces of dried mango for an exotic flavor.

When you add dried fruit to your coffee, you can mix it directly into your cup or use it as a topping. You can also toast them lightly to intensify their flavors. Remember to consider your personal preferences and adjust the quantities to your taste to get the perfect coffee experience.

COMPLEMENTARY FLAVOURS

To enhance your coffee by using complementary flavors, here are some suggestions:

Chocolate : Chocolate and coffee are flavors that complement each other very well. You can add a pinch of cocoa powder or a little chocolate syrup to your coffee for a rich, gourmet flavor.

Vanilla : Vanilla is a classic flavor that goes well with coffee. You can use vanilla extract or vanilla syrup to add a subtle sweetness to your coffee.

Caramel : Caramel adds a sweet and caramelized note to your coffee. You can use caramel syrup for a mild and decadent flavor.

Hazelnut : The flavors of hazelnut and coffee blend harmoniously. Add a little hazelnut syrup or crushed roasted hazelnuts to your coffee for a delicious flavor.

Maple : Maple syrup or maple sugar can add natural sweetness and warm flavor to your coffee.

White chocolate : White chocolate can bring a creamy sweetness and a subtle hint of vanilla to your coffee. Try adding white chocolate chips or white chocolate syrup to your coffee.

Coconut : Coconut can give a tropical touch and a slight sweetness to your coffee. Use coconut milk or coconut cream for a creamy flavor, or sprinkle with roasted coconut shavings on top.

Toasted almond: Toasted almonds bring a delicious nutty flavor and crunchy texture to your coffee. Add toasted sliced almonds to the top of your coffee.

Honey : Honey is a natural alternative to sugar that adds a subtle sweetness and distinct flavor to your coffee. Add a teaspoon of honey and stir well to stir in.

Salted butter : Salted butter can add a rich caramel flavor and salty touch to your coffee. Add a small amount of salted butter and mix until it melts.

These suggestions can help you create interesting combinations by pairing complementary flavors with your coffee. Experiment and adjust the amounts according to your personal preference to get the perfect flavor profile for your cup of coffee.

MILK AND PLANT-BASED ALTERNATIVES: CREATIVE TEXTURES AND FLAVOURS

There are many milks options and plant-based alternatives that you can add to your coffee to enhance it. Here are some suggestions:

Cow's milk : Cow's milk is the most common and traditional option for adding creaminess to your coffee. It can soften the flavor and add a creamy texture.

Almond milk : Almond milk is a popular plant-based alternative for coffee. It has a slightly sweet flavor and lighter texture than cow's milk. It can bring a pleasant nutty note to your coffee.

Oat milk: Oat milk has a creamy texture and mild flavor. It goes well with coffee, adding a slight cereal note and a pleasant creaminess.

Coconut milk : Coconut milk adds tropical flavor and rich creaminess to your coffee. It can be especially delicious in iced coffees or drinks with an exotic taste.

Soy milk: Soy milk is a common and versatile plant-based alternative for coffee. It has a slightly creamy texture and a neutral flavor that pairs well with coffee.

Hazelnut milk : Hazelnut milk adds a delicate nutty flavor and slightly creamy texture to your coffee. It can bring an interesting aromatic note.

Rice milk : Rice milk has a mild and slightly sweet flavor. It has a lighter texture than some other alternatives and can be enjoyed by those who prefer a lighter option.

Hemp milk : Hemp milk has a creamy texture and a subtle nutty flavor. It is rich in nutrients and can be an interesting option for those looking for plant-based alternatives.

Cashew milk: Cashew milk has a creamy texture and a sweet, delicate flavor. It can bring a subtle nutty note to your coffee.

Pistachio milk: Pistachio milk has a distinct flavor and creamy texture. It can add a touch of luxury and richness to your coffee.

Sesame milk : Sesame milk has a slightly toasted flavor and creamy texture. It can bring a unique note to your coffee.

Spelt milk: Spelt milk is a lesser-known alternative, but it has a mild flavor and creamy texture. It can add a subtle nutty note to your coffee.

Quinoa milk: Quinoa milk is naturally sweet and has a slightly finer texture. It can give a unique flavor to your coffee.

Macadamia nut milk: Macadamia nut milk has a rich, creamy flavor. It can bring a luxurious creaminess to your coffee.

Chestnut milk: Chestnut milk has a mild and slightly sweet flavor, with a slight nutty note. It can add an interesting dimension to your coffee.

Remember to choose unsweetened or slightly sweetened options if you prefer to control the amount of sugar in your coffee. Experiment with different alternatives to find the one that best suits your taste preferences and dietary needs.

CAFFEINATED DESSERTS AND DELICACIES

There are plenty of options for desserts and caffeinated treats that you can prepare to accompany your coffee. Here are some ideas:

Affogato: An affogato is a simple but delicious Italian dessert. Pour a hot espresso over a scoop of vanilla ice cream. When hot coffee meets cold ice cream, it creates a delicious combination of flavors.

Tiramisu: Tiramisu is a classic Italian dessert made with biscuits soaked in coffee and creamy mascarpone. It is usually sprinkled with cocoa powder for a finishing touch.

Coffee cookies : Make coffee-flavoured cookies by adding instant coffee or finely ground coffee to your favourite cookie recipe. Coffee cookies are perfect to accompany your cup of coffee.

Coffee muffins : Coffee muffins are a great option for coffee lovers. You can add ground coffee or coffee extract to muffin batter for a caffeinated flavor.

Panna cotta with coffee : Panna cotta is an Italian dessert made with cream, sugar and gelatin. Add strong coffee or coffee extract to the traditional recipe to create a caffeinated version of this dessert.

Coffee brownies : Add instant coffee or finely ground coffee to your brownie recipe to give them a rich, deep coffee flavor.

Coffee crème brûlée : Make a classic crème brûlée with a touch of coffee. The aroma of coffee blends perfectly with the richness of crème brûlée.

Coffee ice cream : Make delicious homemade coffee ice cream by adding finely ground coffee to the base of your favorite ice cream recipe. You can also add pieces of chocolate or cookies for extra flavor.

Iced coffee : Make a refreshing iced coffee by mixing strong coffee with ice cubes, milk or a plant-based alternative, and syrup of your choice. You can add whipped cream and sprinkle cocoa or cinnamon on top for a gourmet touch.

Biscotti with coffee : Biscottis are crunchy Italian cookies that are perfect for dipping in coffee. Add crushed coffee beans or instant coffee to your biscotti recipe for an intense coffee flavor.

Coffee mousse : Make a delicious coffee mousse by mixing strong chilled coffee with whipped cream and sugar. Serve it in individual cups and decorate with chocolate shavings or cocoa powder.

Coffee cake : Make a fluffy, coffee-flavored cake by adding strong coffee and coffee extract to your favorite cake recipe. You can also add ganache to coffee for even more flavor.

Coffee-fruit crumble : Make a fruit crumble by adding a touch of coffee to the fruit filling. The sweet flavors of the fruit will blend perfectly with the roasted flavor of the coffee.

Coffee pancakes : Add finely ground coffee to your pancake batter for deliciously fragrant coffee pancakes. Serve them with maple syrup, whipped cream and fruit for a caffeinated brunch.

Coffee truffles : Make chocolate truffles by adding strong coffee or coffee extract to the ganache. Roll truffles in cocoa powder or ground coffee for a tasty finishing touch.

Coffee popsicles : Mix strong coffee with milk or a plant-based alternative, sugar and vanilla flavors to make coffee popsicles. Perfect for cooling off on hot days.

These suggestions offer you a variety of desserts and caffeinated delicacies to satisfy your palate. Feel free to experiment and adapt the recipes according to your personal preferences.

EXPLORE COFFEE CULTURES AROUND THE WORLD

Coffee is grown in several regions of the world, each making its own contribution to flavor profiles and caffeinated traditions. Here is an overview of coffee crops in different parts of the globe:

Latin America : Latin American countries, such as Brazil, Colombia, Costa Rica and Guatemala, are renowned for their coffee production. These regions offer a wide variety of coffees, ranging from the sweet, chocolatey notes of Brazil to the bright, fruity flavors of Colombia. Coffee culture in

Latin America is deeply rooted in tradition and is an important part of the local economy.

East Africa : Countries such as Ethiopia, Kenya, Tanzania and Rwanda are key players in the coffee industry in East Africa. Ethiopia is often considered the birthplace of coffee, with a long history of growing and consuming the drink. East African coffees are renowned for their bold flavors, floral notes and fruity aromas.

Southeast Asia : Southeast Asian countries, such as Indonesia, Vietnam and Thailand, are major coffee producers. Indonesia is known for its world-famous coffee, Sumatran coffee, which has earthy aromas and low acidity. Vietnam is famous for its robusta coffee, which is often used in the production of instant coffee.

Middle East : In Middle Eastern countries, such as Turkey and Saudi Arabia, coffee occupies a central place in culture and traditions. Turkish coffee, prepared with finely ground coffee and boiled with water, is known for its strong taste and thick texture. Arabic coffee is often flavored with spices like cardamom and is served during traditional welcoming and hospitality ceremonies.

North America : Although coffee production in North America is not as large as in other regions, states like the United States and Canada have a booming coffee culture. Micro-roasters and specialty coffees offer a variety of quality coffees from different parts of the world, with a focus on sustainability and traceability of beans.

Central America : Central American countries such as Honduras, Nicaragua, El Salvador and Panama are reputable coffee producers. These regions offer a variety of flavor profiles, ranging from fruity and tangy notes to sweeter, chocolatey aromas. Central American coffees are often valued for their balance and complexity.

Caribbean : Caribbean islands such as Jamaica, Dominican Republic, Puerto Rico, and Cuba also have a tradition of coffee cultivation. Jamaica is known for its Blue Mountain coffee, considered one of the best coffees in the world because of its subtle notes and sweetness.

Oceania : In the Oceania region, Papua New Guinea, Indonesia (including the island of Java) and Hawaii are major coffee producers. Hawaii is famous for its Kona coffee, which grows in the volcanic regions of the island and offers a smooth, slightly tart taste.

Europe : Although coffee cultivation is not as developed in Europe compared to other regions, some countries have a notable presence. Italy is well known for its love and expertise of coffee, with traditions such as espresso and cappuccino. Countries such as Spain, France and Germany also have well-established coffee cultures, with their own preparation methods and consumption habits.

India : India is a coffee-producing country, with regions such as the states of Karnataka, Kerala and Tamil Nadu known for their coffee production.

India is particularly famous for its robusta coffee, which is used in many coffee blends.

China : Coffee cultivation in China has grown rapidly in recent years. Regions like Yunnan and Hainan produce high-quality specialty coffee, with unique flavors that reflect the local terroir.

Australia and New Zealand : Australia and New Zealand have a vibrant and thriving caffeine scene. Specialty coffees, expert baristas, and unique brewing methods are highly valued in these countries, where coffee is considered a true passion.

Ethiopia : Ethiopia is often considered the birthplace of coffee. It is in this East African country that Arabica coffee originates. Ethiopia has a long tradition of growing and drinking coffee, with traditional coffee ceremonies that are an integral part of Ethiopian culture.

Colombia : Colombia is renowned for its production of high-quality coffee. Colombian regions, such as the department of Antioquia and the Huila coffee region, produce Arabica coffees renowned for their sweet, fruity and balanced notes.

Guatemala : Guatemala is another Central American country that stands out for its specialty coffee production. Guatemalan coffees are appreciated for their complex and balanced flavors, with notes of chocolate, fruit and caramel.

Each region brings its own influence and unique characteristics to the coffee industry, whether through cultivation methods, cultivated coffee varieties or drinking traditions. Discovering coffee cultures around the world is a fascinating adventure that allows you to appreciate the diversity and richness of this beloved drink.

ICONIC ENHANCED COFFEES FROM DIFFERENT REGIONS

Here are some examples of iconic enhanced coffees from different parts of the world:

French latte : Originating in France, café au lait is a combination of filtered coffee or espresso mixed with warm milk. It is a classic and comforting drink, often served at breakfast.

Italian espresso : Italy is famous for its espresso, a method of extracting coffee where hot water is forced through finely ground coffee to produce a small volume of concentrated coffee. Italian espresso is the basis of many drinks such as cappuccino and macchiato.

Turkish coffee : In Turkey, Turkish coffee is an iconic drink. Prepared in a small saucepan called cezve, Turkish coffee is brewed with water and very fine ground coffee. It is served with a creamy foam on top and is often accompanied by sugar or loukoums.

Greek Coffee Frappe : Greek Coffee Frappe is a refreshing and popular drink in Greece. It is prepared by mixing instant coffee with cold water, sugar and ice cubes. Everything is mixed until you get a creamy foam, then served with a straw.

Vietnamese coffee: Vietnamese coffee is a full-bodied, sweet coffee made with finely ground coffee that is brewed into a metal coffee filter placed on a cup containing sweetened condensed milk. Once the coffee has drained, it is mixed with the condensed milk to obtain a creamy and tasty drink.

Spanish coffee : In Spain, Spanish coffee is often served as café con leche, a combination of coffee and hot milk. It's common to find variations flavored with cinnamon or orange peel to add an extra touch of flavor.

Ethiopian coffee : Ethiopia, considered the birthplace of coffee, has a tradition of coffee ceremony. The coffee is roasted and ground by hand, then prepared in a jabena, a traditional ceramic container. The Ethiopian coffee ceremony is an important ritual that involves specific steps and careful presentation.

Italian affogato : Originally from Italy, affogato is a combination of hot espresso coffee poured over a scoop of vanilla ice cream. The warmth of the coffee melts the ice cream, creating a delicious blend of creamy flavors and coffee.

Australian Flat White : Flat White is a coffee drink of Australian and New Zealand origin. It is prepared by pouring a double espresso over warm milk, creating a smooth and velvety texture. Flat White is appreciated for its balance between coffee and milk, without the thick foam of a cappuccino.

Brazilian latte : In Brazil, latte is a popular and traditional drink. It is prepared by mixing filtered coffee with warm milk. Brazilian latte is often eaten at breakfast and can be accompanied by cheese bread or pão de queijo.

Cuban coffee: Cuban coffee, also known as cafecito or espresso coffee, is a powerful and sweet drink. It is prepared by infusing an espresso with sugar, creating a sweet and caramelized flavor. Cuban coffee is often served in small glasses called "tacitas" and is enjoyed at any time of the day.

Italian macchiato coffee: Macchiato coffee is an espresso with a small amount of hot milk "marked" on top. In Italian, "macchiato" means "spotted" or "marked". This drink offers a subtle balance between the intensity of espresso and the sweetness of milk.

Mocha : Mocha is a drink that combines coffee and chocolate. It is prepared by adding chocolate syrup or cocoa powder to an espresso and then adding warm milk to it. Mocha is often topped with whipped cream and chocolate shavings for an extra gourmet touch.

Thai iced coffee: Thai iced coffee, also known as "Thai ced coffee", is a refreshing and sweet drink. It is prepared by mixing strong coffee with sweetened condensed milk, and then pouring it over ice cubes. The drink is often served with a spoon to mix the flavors.

These examples represent some of the iconic enhanced coffees from different parts of the world. Each region has its own preparation methods, ingredients and traditions associated with coffee consumption, creating a unique and distinctive experience.

TRADITIONS AND RITUALS ASSOCIATED WITH COFFEE IN VARIOUS COUNTRIES

Coffee is much more than just a beverage in many countries around the world. It is associated with traditions and rituals that reflect the culture and lifestyle of each region. Here are some examples of traditions and rituals associated with coffee in various countries:

Ethiopian coffee ceremony : In Ethiopia, considered the birthplace of coffee, the coffee ceremony is an important ritual. It often takes place in homes and is a symbol of hospitality. The coffee beans are roasted over an open fire and then ground by hand. Coffee is made in a ceramic container called jabena and served in small cups. The Ethiopian coffee ceremony is a moment of sharing and conviviality, where participants gather to discuss, sing and enjoy coffee.

Italian espresso and coffee rituals : In Italy, espresso is an integral part of everyday life and social interactions. Italians usually have their coffee at the bar, standing at the counter, rather than quickly consuming it to take away. It's common to see Italians having an espresso in the morning and then another after lunch. It's an opportunity to pause, chat and socialize.

Turkish coffee and fortune reading : In Turkey, the preparation and tasting of Turkish coffee is accompanied by a tradition of fortune reading. Once the coffee is drunk, the coffee grounds remaining in the cup are reversed on the saucer. After a short time, the pomace is used to predict the future of the person. A specialist in reading fortune, called "kahveci", interprets the patterns left by coffee grounds to reveal omens and symbols.

Greek coffee and relaxation : In Greece, Greek coffee is often accompanied by a relaxing ritual. Greeks like to take their time to enjoy their coffee, slowly sipping it while chatting with friends or reading a newspaper. It is a moment of pause and conviviality, where we enjoy the coffee and the company of others.

Moroccan coffee and tea ceremony : In Morocco, although mint tea is more popular, coffee also has its place at meetings and special occasions. Moroccan coffee is often prepared in a brass coffee maker called "kanoun" and served in small cups. It is often accompanied by traditional Moroccan pastries and moments of sharing.

Brazilian coffee and lively atmosphere : In Brazil, coffee is deeply rooted in culture and traditions. Brazilians are used to having their coffee in groups, at family gatherings or with friends. It is a festive time when coffee is served in abundance, accompanied by cakes, cookies and lively conversations.

Vietnamese coffee and filtering through the drip filter : In Vietnam, coffee is often prepared using a metal drip filter, called a "phin". The ground coffee is placed in the filter, and then hot water is slowly poured over it. Coffee flows drop by drop into a cup or glass containing sweetened condensed milk. This ritual of filtering and slow tasting is appreciated for its simplicity and sweetness.

Japanese coffee and siphon coffee ceremony : In Japan, siphon coffee is a method of preparation that is considered an art form. The siphon device uses steam pressure to extract coffee precisely, creating a clean, aromatic drink. The siphon coffee ceremony is a visual spectacle, where the barista is often dressed in traditional attire and prepares coffee with great precision.

American coffee and coffee breaks : In the United States, the coffee break is an essential part of the workday. Americans like to have a cup of coffee to take a break and recharge their energy. Cafes are often equipped with self-service coffee machines, allowing people to serve themselves and customize their coffee according to their preferences.

South African coffee and drinking together : In South Africa, coffee is often associated with the concept of "ubuntu", which means "I am because we are". South Africans enjoy sharing a cup of coffee with family, friends or colleagues, creating moments of connection and sharing.

Arabic coffee and hospitality : In many Arab countries, coffee is a symbol of hospitality. Guests greet their guests with fragrant Arabic coffee, often flavored with cardamom. Coffee is served in small cups, and guests are encouraged to drink at least one to show appreciation.

Indian coffee and masala chai: In India, coffee is less common than tea, but masala chai, a spicy milk tea, is very popular. However, in some parts of South India, filter coffee is prepared in the traditional way and is often enjoyed with small snacks like dosas and idlis.

Swedish coffee and "Fika" break : In Sweden, the coffee break is an important tradition called "Fika". Swedes often take a break in the afternoon to relax with a cup of coffee and pastries, such as cinnamon rolls or cookies. It is a moment of conviviality where people meet to discuss and recharge their batteries.

Moroccan coffee and traditional coffee ceremony : In Morocco, coffee preparation is a ceremony in itself. The coffee is finely ground by hand and boiled in a small copper coffee pot called "berrad", then poured into small glass cups called "tchakbatt". It is often flavored with spices like cardamom or cinnamon and served with dates.

Norwegian coffee and "Kos" : In Norway, coffee is associated with the concept of "Kos", which means feeling comfortable and enjoying a moment of relaxation. Norwegians like to have their coffee with snacks or cakes, while enjoying the company of their loved ones. It's an opportunity to slow down and savor the moment.

Bedouin coffee and ritual hospitality : In Bedouin culture, coffee is a symbol of hospitality. The coffee is finely ground by hand, boiled with water and sometimes flavored with spices like cardamom. The coffee is then served to guests in small cups, usually three cups, with gestures of respect and generosity.

Indonesian coffee and "Kopi Luwak" : In Indonesia, Kopi Luwak coffee is considered a specialty. This coffee is produced from coffee beans that have been eaten and excreted by the civet, a small weasel-like animal. The recovered beans are then cleaned, roasted and transformed into a beverage prized for its unique flavors.

Malian coffee and "bistro" ceremony : In Mali, coffee is often prepared in a terracotta coffee pot called a "bistrot". Coffee preparation is a slow and methodical process, where coffee is boiled several times to obtain a thick, aromatic drink. Malian coffee is often accompanied by music and dance during celebrations and gatherings.

These examples show how coffee is steeped in traditions and rituals in different cultures around the world. These practices add a social and cultural dimension to coffee consumption, creating moments of sharing, conviviality and relaxation.

DISCOVER LOCAL CAFES ON TRIPS

When you travel, discovering local cafes can be a rewarding experience that allows you to explore the unique culture and flavors of a region. Here are some tips to help you discover local cafes on your travels:

Look for independent coffee shops : Avoid large international coffee chains and opt for local independent cafes instead. These cafes are often hidden gems, offering authentic experiences and unique flavors. Research online, check travel guides, or ask locals for recommendations to find the best independent cafes in the area you're visiting.

Explore local neighborhoods : Local cafes tend to be found in bustling, trendy neighborhoods, away from traditional tourist areas. Take time to venture into the local neighborhoods, where you'll often find quaint cafes and cozy atmospheres. You might also have the opportunity to discover cafes nestled in charming alleys or courtyards.

Talk to locals : Locals are often the most knowledgeable about the best cafes in their city. Feel free to strike up a conversation with locals, such as your accommodation employees, taxi drivers, or local shopkeepers. They will be happy to share their personal recommendations and guide you to the most popular local cafes in the area.

Participate in coffee tastings : In some regions, coffee tastings are held, where you can learn about the different varieties of coffee, preparation methods, and unique flavor profiles. Look for coffee shops or roasting workshops that offer coffee tasting sessions, where you can expand your knowledge and palate.

Try the local specialties : Each region has its own coffee specialties. When you visit a local coffee shop, try their iconic drinks or special brewing methods. For example, in Turkey, try Turkish coffee prepared in a cezve, or in Vietnam, try Vietnamese coffee made with sweetened condensed milk.

Be open to new experiences : When discovering local cafes, be prepared to step out of your comfort zone and try new flavors and combinations. Some regions may offer coffees with unexpected ingredients or unique preparation methods. Be adventurous and be surprised by the discoveries you will make.

Discovering local cafes on your travels allows you to have a more authentic experience and taste the unique flavors of each region. Whether you're a coffee lover or just curious, exploring local cafes is a way to connect with a place's culture and traditions through a cup of coffee.

THANKS

Dear reader,

At the end of this fascinating journey through the world of enhanced coffees, I would like to express my deep gratitude to all those who contributed to the realization of "Magic Coffee: Bewitching Aromas to Awaken Your Senses".

First of all, I thank the baristas, coffee artisans and tasting experts who generously shared their passion and know-how. Their expertise and valuable advice have enriched the pages of this book and have created unique caffeinated experiences.

Creative Consciousness Editions   Kris Roots

I would also like to thank the coffee farmers around the world, who with their dedication and know-how, grow exceptional beans. Their iconic coffees inspired our research and fueled our love for the drink.

A big thank you to my loved ones, who supported my project with enthusiasm and encouragement. Your unwavering support has been an inexhaustible source of inspiration.

Finally, I address my most sincere thanks to you, dear readers. It is thanks to your curiosity and interest in the world of coffee that this book comes to life. I sincerely hope that you will find in these pages the inspiration and creativity to elevate your caffeinated experience to new heights.

Let each sip of coffee transport you to unexplored taste horizons and awaken your senses with enchantment.

Yours sincerely,

Kris Roots

Copyright © 2023 Kris Roots' Creative Consciousness Editions

Creative Consciousness Editions   Kris Roots